Python Programming for Beginners

D1528541

Introduction

I want to thank you and congratulate you for downloading the book, "Python Programming for Beginners".

This book contains the steps, strategies, and information you need to learn the fundamentals of Python Programming rapidly and effortlessly. It provides a solid foundation for self-learners who are learning programming for the first time and an excellent resource material for experienced programmers who want to expand their horizon and tap the powerful features of Python.

Python Programming for Beginners explores the nature and features of Python as a programming language. It offers a step-by-step guide to help you understand and master its syntax, commands, data types, functions, and its many useful modules.

It uses a practical and straightforward approach that will appeal to most users who have less time to digest technical jargons and fluff. It provides relevant examples that are specifically created to make learning Python an enjoyable and worthwhile experience.

Thanks again for downloading this book, I hope you enjoy it!

Table of Contents

Chapter 1
Getting to Know Python

Python is a general purpose programming language that is powerful and versatile. It supports several programming paradigms such as object-oriented, aspect-oriented, functional, and structured.

It is an interpreted language. It converts human codes into machine-readable byte codes before it can execute them.

Python was developed by Guido van Rossum in the late 1980s. He derived much of its syntax from ABC and C programming languages.

It is one of the most widely used programming languages for beginners. It implements simple syntax rules that make Python programs appear like blocks of regular English expressions. It is a high level programming language that is quick and easy to learn and master.

Python is built with extensive libraries that enable programmers to create large, practical, and meaningful programs in a short span of time.

Learning Python can give you a solid foundation for a rewarding programming career.

Chapter 2
Installing Python and Using IDLE

How to Install Python

Python is an open source language that is free to use and distribute for both personal and commercial use. Python Software Foundation is the administrator of Python and you can download its installation files from its website.

How to Install Python in Windows

For Windows OS users, you can download the installation package for your preferred version though this link:

https://www.python.org/downloads/

There are two main versions to choose from - the latest version of Python 3, 3.5.2, and the latest version of Python 2, 2.7.12. You can find older versions by scrolling down the page.

After downloading the package, just run the installation files by clicking on its icon. You may choose to customize the installation by specifying the location and features and deciding whether you want the installation to be for the current user or for all users of the computer. Otherwise, you can just install using default settings.

How to Install Python in Mac

Mac users can download Python's installation package using this link:

https://www.python.org/downloads/mac-osx/

How to Install Python in UNIX/Linux

UNIX or Linux users can download the installation package using this link:

https://www.python.org/downloads/source/

You can install Python by clicking on the downloaded installation file. An installation package includes IDLE, pip, and documentation.

Starting Python

There are at least two ways to start Python: though the command line terminal or through IDLE. The command line features a basic interface that will allow you to try out bits of codes and run your program. IDLE, which stands for Integrated Development Learning Environment, is an IDE which is created exclusively for Python.

Windows users can start the command line or IDLE by clicking on the menu item or its icon on the Start menu. You may also access the folder containing the installation files or a shortcut to the installation files and click on the Python Interactive Shell (command line) or IDLE.

Mac and GNU/Linux UNIX users will have to run the Terminal Tool and enter Python to start a session.

Using IDLE

IDLE provides standard graphical user interface with many helpful features that make writing Python programs intuitive and efficient. It is a flexible platform that you can use on either script mode or interactive mode.

When used in the interactive mode, Python evaluates each expression entered as it simultaneously executes previous expressions stored in active memory. It provides instant feedback after reading the last expression entered. This mode is typically used to test program segments. It is quite useful for learning Python's syntax.

When used in the script mode, also called the standard mode, the interpreter runs Python scripts or files saved with a .py extension.

IDLE features the Python Shell, multiple window text editor, smart indentation, auto-completion, syntax highlighting, and an integrated debugger.

The Python Shell

The Python Shell uses a drop down menu with many useful features. You will use the prompt on the Shell to work interactively with Python by simply entering an expression. Unlike the basic command line, you can copy-paste expressions on previous rows and use them on the current row.

The Python Shell has the following options on its main menu:

File
Edit
Shell
Debug
Options
Windows
Help

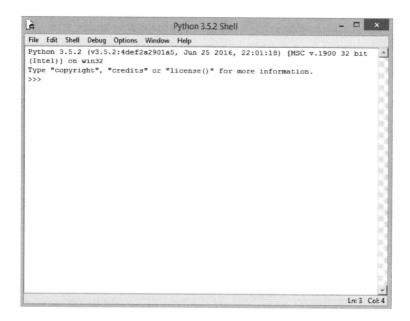

The File Menu

The File menu lets you create a new file, open a saved file or module, save a new file or copy, save a file under a different name, search for and open a class, browse sys.path, close current file, print and save the present window, and exit Python Shell.

Clicking on the 'New File' under the File menu opens a built-in text editor with almost the same menu as the Python Shell. You will use this text editor to write and save your program or modules, check and run them, and display the output on the Python Shell. The menu options for the text editor are File, Edit, Format, Run, Options, Windows, and Help.

Writing and Running a Python Program

To write a program, you can use the integrated text editor or other text editors. Programs written and saved in the built-in text editor automatically takes a .py extension while those written in other platforms should be saved with a .py extension.

Using the Integrated Text Editor

To access the built-in text editor on Python Shell, you have to click on File and choose New File.

Next, you can write a simple program that will print a string:

print('Python Programming is Fun!')

When you're done, you need to save the file. You can save it in the current working directory or in any folder of your choice

To save: Click on File, choose Save

The Save option opens a Save as dialogue box that will let you name the file and the destination folder. Save the file as MyFirstProgram on the default folder.

Running the Program

To run your program, click on the Run module option on the text editor's Run Menu. If there are no errors, you should see the following on Python Shell:

```
=======RESTART: C: /Python/MyFirstProgram.py
=======
```

Python Programming is Fun!

Chapter 3
Files and Directories

Python manages files and directories through its os module. The os module contains several useful methods and functions for creating, modifying, or removing directories.

mkdir() method

The mkdir() method is used to create a new directory. It takes one argument, the new directory name.

syntax:

os.mkdir("new_dir")

For example, to create a new directory named 'new' on drive c:

import os
os.mkdir('c:\\specialprogs')

chdir() method

The chdir() method is used when you need to work on a file which is stored in another directory. It takes one argument: the name of the directory that you want to use.

syntax:
os.chdir('new_dir')

For example, if you are currently working on a file stored in the folder C:/Programs/Python/Apps and you want to use a file stored in the folder c:/New, you will change the working directory with the following statements:

```
import os
os.chdir("c:\\New")
```

getcwd()

The current working directory is the folder stored in the active memory of Python. When you enter expressions such as 'import file.txt', Python locates the file in the current working directory. The getcwd() method is used to obtain the current working directory.

syntax:

```
os.getcwd()
```

Example:

```
import os
os.getcwd()
'C:\\New'
```

rmdir()

The rmdir() method is used to remove a folder. It takes one argument: the name of the folder to be deleted. A folder must first be emptied of files before it can be deleted.

syntax:

```
os.rmdir('dir_name')
```

Example:

```python
import os
os.rmdir('c:\\New')
```

Chapter 4
Python Syntax

Programming syntax refers to the set of rules that define how programs should be written and how they are to be interpreted.

Keywords

Keywords are reserved words that Python uses for its processes and built-in functions. To avoid programming errors, the following keywords should not be used as an identifier when naming Python objects:

class	for	continue
True	False	None
finally	try	lambda
return	from	is
global	while	def
and	not	del
nonlocal	as	with
elif	or	if
except	break	yield
import	raise	else
pass	in	assert

Identifiers

An identifier is a name given to Python objects such as variables, classes, modules, and functions. You should take note of the following rules and conventions when naming objects:

An identifier can be a combination of uppercase and lowercase letters, an underscore, or digit. It should not start with a digit.

An identifier should not contain a special character such as &, %, #, or $.

You can use underscores to connect multiple-word identifiers.

Python is case-sensitive.

Examples of Valid Identifiers:

Variable_1, employees, my_grading_sheet, CamelCaseName

Examples of Invalid identifiers:
6variable, key@

Quotation Marks

A pair of single ('), double ("), or triple (''') quotation marks are used to indicate string literals in Python.

Examples:

'Name', "Beatriz", '''Branch: ''', 'Enter a number: '

Statements

Statements are expressions written inside a program which are read, ignored, or run by the interpreter. Python supports statements such as if, for, while, break, continue, pass, and assignment statements.

Multiple-line statements

A multiple-line statement is a single statement that spans several lines. You can indicate implicitly that a multi-line statement is a single statement by wrapping the lines inside parentheses (), square brackets [] or curly braces {}.

Example:

```
>>> alphabet = ('a', 'b', 'c', 'd', 'e', 'f', 'g'
                'h', 'i', 'j', 'k', 'l', 'm', 'n'
                'o', 'p', 'q', 'r', 's', 't', 'u'
                'v', 'w', 'x', 'y', 'z')
```

To explicitly indicate continuity, you can use a backslash at the end of each line:

```
>>> letters = ["a", "b", "c", "d", "e", "f", "g", \
               "h", "i", "j", "k", "l", "m", "n", \
               "o", "p", "q", "r", "s", "t"]
```

Indentation

Python strictly implements indentation to structure its programs. All statements in a block of code start from the same point going to the right. A nested code is indicated by a deeper indentation. By convention, programmers apply 4 white spaces instead of tabs.

Comments

Programmers typically write comments inside the program to describe a process or provide important information. Comments enhance program documentation. In Python, a hash # symbol is used before a comment to tell the interpreter to ignore the line.

Example:

#This program computes for weekly salary.

A comment can span over several lines. To wrap them together, you can use a # symbol at the beginning of each line.

Example:

#This is a long
#comment that spans
#over several lines

You can also wrap multi-line comments with a pair of triple quotes (""").

Example:

"""This is a long
comment that spans
over several lines"""

Docstring

A documentation string or docstring is used to describe and document what a function or a class does. It is written at the top of a block of code that defines or names a function, class, or module. A docstring is typically written as a phrase that starts in an uppercase and ends with a period. It is commonly a one-line statement that is written in an imperative form and is enclosed by a pair of triple quotes (""").

Examples:

```python
def triple_value(num):
    """Function to get thrice the value of a number."""
    return 3*num
```

Chapter 5
Variables

Variables

A variable is a reserved memory location that is used to store and access value. It is given a unique name to identify its location and to allow users to access the stored data.

Compared to most computer languages, creating a variable is more flexible and straightforward in Python. You can easily declare and reassign a variable with an assignment operator (=). There is no syntax requirement for declaring the data type because the interpreter intuitively identifies the data type of the value assigned.

Examples of variable assignment statements:

employee = "John Snorkel"
number = 30
average = 90.5
remark = "Needs improvement."

The left operand is the identifier for the variable while the right operand is the value assigned to each variable. The assignment operator indicates that a variable is set to a particular value.

Python allows several assignments in one statement. In such cases, the values are assigned according to their positional order.

Example:

x, y, z = 15, 14, "normal"

Likewise, Python allows you to you assign one value to several variables in one assignment statement.

Example:

x = y = z = 32

The statement assigns the integer 32 to variables a, b, and c simultaneously. You can use the id() operator to verify if all variables refer to the same memory location.

>>> id(x)
1636784896

>>> id(y)
1636784896

>>> id(z)
1636784896

Reassigning a variable is as easy as using the variable name in another assignment statement.

For example, if you want to reassign variable x above to the string 'land forms', you can make another assignment statement:

>>> x = 'land forms'

To check out its new memory location:

>>> id(x)
59030768

Chapter 6
Data Types

Programming involves working with different types of data or objects. These data may be built-in, defined by users, or imported from internal and external modules or libraries.

Python supports the following basic data types:

- numbers
- string
- list
- tuple
- dictionary

Numbers

There are three numeric data types in Python 3:

integers
floating point numbers or floats
complex numbers

Integers

An integer is a whole number that has no decimal point or fractional part. It can have unlimited size in Python 3 and includes zero, positive, or negative numbers.

Normal integers

Examples: 25, 0, -40, 98746532581717

Binary literal (base 2)

A binary literal is prefixed by zero (0) and an uppercase B or lowercase b:

Example:

```
>>> 0b0010
2
```

Octal literal (base 8)

An octal literal is introduced by zero (0) and uppercase O or lowercase o.

Examples:

```
>>> 0O20
16
```

```
>>> 0o20
16
```

```
>>> oct_lit = 0O20
>>> print(oct_lit)
16
```

Hexadecimal literal (base 16)

A hexadecimal literal is prefixed by zero (0) and an uppercase X or lowercase x.

Examples:

```
>>> 0xa0f
```

2575

>>> 0XA0F
2575

Converting Integers to String

The built-in functions bin(), oct(), and hex() are used to convert an integer to its literal representation.

For example, to convert the integer 25 to its binary, octal, and hexadecimal literals:

integer to binary literal:
>>> bin(25)
'0b11001'

integer to octal literal:
>>> oct(25)
'0o31'

integer to hexadecimal literal
>>> hex(25)
'0x19'

Floating-Point Numbers

A floating point number or float is a real number with a decimal point and fractional part.

Examples: 50.75, 10.5, 76864800976.25

Complex Number

A complex number is a pair of a real and an imaginary number. It takes the form 'a+bj' or 'a+bJ' where 'a' and 'b' are floats and 'J' or 'j' is an imaginary number which signifies the square root of -1.

Example:

```
>>> a = 5 + 4j
>>> b = 2 - 3j
>>> ab = a + b
>>> print(ab)
(7+1j)
```

Converting One Numeric Type to Another

Syntax may sometimes require the explicit conversion of a number to another. You can compel Python to make the conversion with the appropriate keyword.

Examples:

Integer to a float:
```
>>> float(15)
15.0
```

Integer to a complex number:
```
>>> complex(5)
(5+0j)
```

A pair of numbers to a complex number:
```
>>> complex(3,2)
(3+2j)
```

A float to an integer:
>>>int(12.25)
12

A float to a complex number:
>>> complex(15.5)
(15.5+0j)

__String__

A string is an ordered series of Unicode characters. It is an immutable data type that may consist of letters, numbers, symbols, or their combination. Strings are enclosed in a pair of single or double quotation marks.

Examples of string assignments:

>>> company = 'Starbright Agency'
>>> job = 'programmer'
>>> name = 'Murphy James'

A string enclosed in a single quote may sometimes have to use a single quotation mark within the string. To avoid syntax error, you must escape the single quote within the string with a backlash symbol (\). The same rule applies when you need to use double quotation marks within a string enclosed in a pair of double quotes.

Examples:

>>> conclusion = 'I can\'t recommend the brand.'
>>>print(conclusion)
I can't recommend the brand.

```
>>> comment = "She answered without hesitation:  \"I'm
going to resign if my father is proven guilty by an
independent court.\""
>>> print(comment)
She answered without hesitation:  "I'm going to resign if my
father is proven guilty by an independent court."
```

How to Access Strings

Indexing

The index operator [] can be used to access strings and their substrings. In Python, the first substring or character has zero as index and the rest of the numbers going to the right are indexed sequentially.

For example, if you set a variable 'place' to the string 'hospital', here's how you will access specific substrings:

```
>>> place = 'hospital'
>>> place[0]
'h'
>>> place[3]
'p'
>>> place[7]
'l'
```

Python likewise supports negative indexing which you can use to access the last substring.

For example, to access the last character in the above string:

```
>>> place[-1]
'l'
```

The built-in len() function is another way to access the last substring. This function is used to obtain the size of the string, that is, the number of characters in a string. To use the len() function to find the last substring, you will have to subtract 1 from its value.

syntax: string[len(string)-1]

Applying this syntax to the above example:

>>> place[len(place)-1]
'l'

Slicing Strings

The slicing operator [:] is used to instruct the interpreter to return a substring from a given string. It takes a maximum of two indices – the first one to indicate the initial substring and the last one to indicate the index of the string to be excluded from the desired substring.

To illustrate, create a new string:

>>> my_string = "requirements"

To access the 5th to the 7th substring on indices 4 to 6:
>>> my_string[4:7]
'ire'

To access the 8th to the 10th substring on indices 7 to 9:
>>> my_string[7:10]
'men'

If your desired substring starts from the initial substring, you may choose to drop the first index. Hence:
```
>>> my_string[:7]
'require'
```

If you want to access a substring that ends with the last substring, you can choose to omit the last index:

```
>>> my_string[7:]
'ments'
```

If you omit both the initial and final index, Python will return the whole string:
```
>>> my_string[:]
'requirements'
```

Likewise, you can use the slicing operator with the + operator to concatenate substrings:

```
>>> my_string[0:2] + my_string[9:]
'rents'
```


How to Concatenate Strings

You can combine two or more strings into a single string with the + operator.

For example:

```
>>> a = 'islands'
>>> b = 'beaches'
>>> 'Exotic ' + a + ' and ' + b + ' are popular vacation destinations.'
'Exotic islands and beaches are popular vacation destinations.'
```

How to Repeat a String

A string or its concatenation may be repeated using the * operator and a number that will indicate the number of times it will be repeated.

For instance, to repeat the string (*_*) three times:

```
>>> '(*_*)'*3
'(*_*)(*_*)(*_*)'
```

Using the upper() method and lower() method on Strings

The upper() method is used to display a string in uppercase while the lower() method is used to display a string in lowercase().

To illustrate, create a variable 'string_1' to hold the string 'Pacific':

```
>>> string_1 = 'Pacific'
```

To return string_1 in uppercase:

```
>>> print(string_1.upper())
PACIFIC
```

This time, display string_1 in lowercase:

```
>>> print(string_1.lower())
pacific
```

You have learned to slice, concatenate, and display strings in uppercase or lowercase. Take note that these operations do not affect the string stored in a variable because, as mentioned, strings are immutable. For example, if you print string_1 at this point:

>>> print(string_1)
Pacific

List

A list is a mutable sequence data type that can hold any number and types of data. Since it is mutable, you can add, edit, sort, or delete any of its elements.

A Python list is distinguished by surrounding square brackets [].

To create an empty list:

my_list = []

To build a list with elements, you will use a comma to separate each item:

my_list = [item_01, item_02, item_03]

Examples of list creation expressions:

food_list = ["French toast", "chicken dumpling", "corn muffins", "pizza"]
num_list = [3, 2, 9, 1, 7, 5]
mixed = ["craps", 65.5, 3]
nested_list = ["poker", 1, 2.75, [9, 7, 5, 1, 3, 4.5]]

Accessing List Elements

There are several ways to access Python's list items:

Indexing

The index operator [] is used to access items on a list as in other sequence data types like strings and tuples. The first element takes the zero index. Attempting to access an index that is beyond the list's index range will return an IndexError.

Examples:

>>>sports = ["baseball", "basketball", "hockey", "soccer", "rugby", "tennis"]

To access the indices 1, 3, and 5:

>>> sports[1]
'basketball'

>>> sports[3]
'soccer'

>>> sports[5]
'tennis'

>>> sports[-1]
'tennis'

If you try to access a non-existent index on the sports list, Python will return an IndexError:

>>> sports[8]
Traceback (most recent call last):
  File "<pyshell#15>", line 1, in <module>

```
    sports[8]
IndexError: list index out of range
```

To access a nested list, you will use nested indexing:

Example:

```
>>> a_list = ["baseball", 12, 8.5, [3, 6, 1, 9, 12]]

>>> a_list[2]
8.5

>>> a_list[3]
[3, 6, 1, 9, 12]

>>> a_list[3][2]
1

>>> a_list[3][-1]
12
```

Slicing Lists

The slicing operator [:] is used to access a range of elements on a list.

For example, create a new list with the following elements:

```
>>> list_1 = ['chameleons', 'lizard', 'snake', 'dinosaur', 'turtle']
```

To access the 2nd (index 1) and 3rd (index 2) element on list_1:

```
>>> list_1[1:3]
```

['lizard', 'snake']

To access the 1st, 2nd, and 3rd element on the list:
>>> list_1[:3]
['chameleons', 'lizard', 'snake']

To access the 2nd up to the last element:
>>> list_1[1:]
['lizard', 'snake', 'dinosaur', 'turtle']

Adding Elements to a List

The append() or extend() methods are used to add elements to an existing list. The append() method is used when you want to add one element. The extend() method is used to add several elements.

syntax:

list.append(x)
list.extend([])

To illustrate, create a list of even numbers:

>>> even_num = [4, 6, 10, 16, 24, 34]

Add another even number, 46, to even_num list using the append method:

>>> even_num.append(46)

To view the updated list:

>>> print(even_num)

[4, 6, 10, 16, 24, 34, 46]

Using the extend() method, add a list of even numbers to even_num:

>>> even_num.extend([48, 50, 52, 54])

To view the updated list:

>>> print(even_num)
[4, 6, 10, 16, 24, 34, 46, 48, 50, 52, 54]

Changing List Elements

The elements of a list can be modified using the indexing [] and assignment (=) operators.

For example, to change the first element of the even_num list from 4 to 2:

>>> even_num[0]= 2

To display the updated even_num list:

>>> print(even_num)
[2, 6, 10, 16, 24, 34, 46, 48, 50, 52, 54]

To replace several elements on the list, you can specify an index range and provide a list of the new elements.

For example, to replace numbers 34, 46, and 48 on the list:

>>> even_num[5:8] = [26, 28, 30]

To view the updated list:

```
>>> even_num
[2, 6, 10, 16, 24, 26, 28, 30, 50, 52, 54]
```

Concatenating and Repeating Lists

Two combine two or more lists, you will use the + operator. You may also use the * operator to indicate the number of times that a list will be repeated.

To illustrate, create two lists:

```
>>> colors = ['yellow', 'blue', 'red', 'purple', 'pink']
>>> shapes = ['diamond', 'circle', 'heart', 'triangle', 'square']
```

Combine the lists colors and shapes under one list:

```
>>> kinder = colors + shapes
```

To view the combined lists:

```
>>> kinder
['yellow', 'blue', 'red', 'purple', 'pink', 'diamond', 'circle',
'heart', 'triangle', 'square']
```

To repeat the colors list thrice:

```
>>> colors * 3
['yellow', 'blue', 'red', 'purple', 'pink', 'yellow', 'blue', 'red',
'purple', 'pink', 'yellow', 'blue', 'red', 'purple', 'pink']
```

Inserting List Elements

The insert() method is used to insert an element on a specified location within the list.

syntax:
list.insert(index, object)

Index refers to the intended index of the item to be inserted while the object is the item to be inserted.

For example, create a list of integers:
>>> int_list = [1, 3, 4, 6, 7, 9]

To insert 2 on index 1:
>>> int_list.insert(1, 2)

To view the modified int_list:
>>> int_list
[1, 2, 3, 4, 6, 7, 9]

Removing or Deleting Items from a List

The remove() and pop() methods are used to remove a single element on a list. The remove() method is used to remove a named item while the pop() method is used to remove the item at a given index.

Syntax for the remove() method:

list.remove(object)

For example, create a new list:

>>> fruits = ['grapes', 'orange', 'yellow', 'apple', 'pear', 'pineapple', 'banana', 'pomelo']

To remove the odd item from the list, namely, 'yellow' using the remove() method:

>>> fruits.remove('yellow')

To display the updated fruits list:
>>> fruits
['grapes', 'orange', 'apple', 'pear', 'pineapple', 'banana', 'pomelo']

The pop() method is used to remove an item on a specified index. When no argument is provided, the method removes the last element on the list. In both cases, it returns the removed item.

syntax:
list.pop()

For example, if you want to delete 'pear', the fourth item on the list:

>>> fruits.pop(3)
'pear'

To view the updated fruits list:

>>> fruits
['grapes', 'orange', 'apple', 'pineapple', 'banana', 'pomelo']

To see what happens if you don't specify an index:

>>> fruits.pop()
'pomelo'

The pop() method removed and returned the last item on the list. Here's the updated fruits list:

```
>>> fruits
['grapes', 'orange', 'apple', 'pineapple', 'banana']
```

You can use the clear() method to empty the fruits list in a single statement:

```
>>> fruits.clear()
>>> fruits
[]
```

The del keyword can likewise be used to delete one or more elements on a list.

syntax
del list[index]

To delete a range of elements:

del list[:]

To illustrate, create a list:

```
>>> my_list = ['peppermint', 'chamomile', 'lavender', 'lemon', 'cocoa', 'eucalyptus']
```

To delete the last item on the list:

```
>>> del my_list[-1]
```

To view the modified list:
```
>>> my_list
['peppermint', 'chamomile', 'lavender', 'lemon', 'cocoa']
```

To delete the elements on index 3 and up:

```
>>> del my_list[3:]
```

To view the remaining items on my_list:
```
>>> print(my_list)
['peppermint', 'chamomile', 'lavender']
```

Another way to remove one or more items on a list is by assigning an empty list to their corresponding index range.

For example, to remove the 2nd and 3rd remaining items on my_list;

```
>>> my_list[1:] = []
```

To view the remaining item on my_list:
```
>>> my_list
['peppermint']
```

Sorting List Elements

The sort() method is used to sort elements of similar data types in an ascending order.

syntax:
list.sort()

For example, here's a list of names:

```
>>> names = ['Matthew', 'Brad', 'Jack', 'Hugh', 'Arriane', 'Jane']
```

To sort the list elements:
```
>>> names.sort()
```

To view the sorted list:

```
>>> names
['Arriane', 'Brad', 'Hugh', 'Jack', 'Jane', 'Matthew']
```

The list is currently arranged in an ascending order. If you want to sort the list and arrange them in descending order, you may use the reverse() method.

syntax:
list.reverse()

For example, to sort the names list on reverse:

```
>>> names.reverse()
```

Here's the updated names list:
```
>>> names
['Matthew', 'Jane', 'Jack', 'Hugh', 'Brad', 'Arriane']
```

The count() method

The count() method is used to return the number of list elements that match a specified element.

Example:

```
>>> numbers = [2, 0, 1, 5, 7, 2, 3, 5, 9, 2, 8, 10]

>>> numbers.count(2)
3
>>> numbers.count(10)
1
>>> numbers.count(5)
2
```

Tuple

A tuple is an immutable sequence data type that can hold an unlimited collection of different data types.

A tuple looks list a list except for its distinguishing round brackets enclosure.

Examples of tuple assignment statements:

numbers = (8, 3, 1, 6, 0, 5, 4)
data = ("work experience", "a", "box")
mixed_tup = (8, 23.25, 0, "checks")
nested_tup = ("blue", (3, 9.5, "x"), [1, 7, 5])
empty_tup = ()

While a tuple typically consists of two or more elements, Python allows the creation of a tuple with only one item. To distinguish a one-item tuple from a string, a comma should immediately follow the item.

For example:

land = ("valley",)

While a pair of square brackets is indispensable to a list, you can create a tuple without the parentheses:

>>> odd = 5, 13, 1, 9, 3

Accessing Tuple Items

Python provides different ways to access a tuple.

Indexing

Accessing tuple items through indexing is similar to how you access list items through indexing.

For example, create a new tuple:

>>> allied = ('nursing', 'dentistry', 'medicine', 'biology', 'veterinary')

To access different indices on the allied tuple:

>>> allied[0]
'nursing'

>>> allied[-1]
'veterinary'

>>> allied[1:4]
('dentistry', 'medicine', 'biology')

>>> allied[0:2]
('nursing', 'dentistry')

>>> allied[2:]
('medicine', 'biology', 'veterinary')

Slicing

Slicing can also be used to access a range of tuple elements.

For example, create a new tuple:

>>> buzzword = ('a', 'g', 'r', 'e', 'e', 'm', 'e', 'n', 't')

To access the item on index 5 and 6:

>>> buzzword[5:7]

('m', 'e')

To access the items on indices zero to the 4th:
>>> buzzword[:5]
('a', 'g', 'r', 'e', 'e')

To access the elements from the index 5 onwards:
>>> buzzword[5:]
('m', 'e', 'n', 't')

Modifying Tuples

A tuple is immutable and in general, you cannot modify its elements. If it contains a mutable element, however, such as a list, you can modify any item or items on that nested list.

For example:

>>> mixed = ('purple', 12, 20.5, [3, 2, 5, 7, 4])

To access the item on index 3, a nested list, and the item on the index 2 of the nested list and replace it with the integer 10:

>>> mixed[3][2]= 10

To view the modified tuple:
>>> mixed
('purple', 12, 20.5, [3, 2, 10, 7, 4])

Reassigning Tuples

It is not always possible to modify tuple items. You can, however, reassign a tuple with a different set of elements.

For example, you can reassign mixed with:

>>> mixed = ('apple pie', 'burger', 'meringue', 'upside down cake')

To view the elements stored in view:

>>> mixed
('apple pie', 'burger', 'meringue', 'upside down cake')

Deleting Tuples

The del keyword can be used to delete a tuple.

syntax:
del tuple

To delete mixed tuple:

del mixed

Python Tuple Methods

There are only two methods that can be used with Python: the count() and index() methods.

count()

The count() method returns the number of elements that matches the given element.

syntax:

tuple.count()

Example:
```
>>> tup = ('r', 'e', 's', 'p', 'o', 'n', 's', 'i', 'b', 'l', 'e')

>>> tup.count('e')
2
>>> tup.count('s')
2
>>> tup.count('l')
1
```

index()

The use of the index() method on a tuple returns the index of the first item that is equal to the given element.

syntax:

tuple.index(x)

For example, create a new tuple:

```
>>> a = ('a', 'r', 'r', 'a', 'n', 'g', 'e')
```

To get the index of the first occurrence of the letter 'a':
```
>>> a.index('a')
0
```

To obtain the index of the first occurrence of 'r':

```
>>> a.index('r')
1
```

To get the index of the first occurrence of 'n':

```
>>> a.index('n')
4
```

Dictionary

A dictionary contains an unordered pairs of keys and values that are connected by a colon (:) and surrounded by curly braces {}. Its key is an immutable data type which means that it can only be a number, string, or tuple. Its value is mutable and can be of any data type.

You can only access a value by accessing its key. A key can only occur once in a dictionary.

Examples of dictionary creation statements:

```
my_dict = {}
sandra = {'Name':'Sandra Chavez', 'age':16, 'State':'Illinois'}
members = {'Name1':'Donna', 'Name2':'Maxene', 'Name3':'Rand'}
```

Accessing Dictionary Items

A dictionary is not an ordered pair. Hence, it is not indexed. To access the data, you have to use the corresponding dictionary key and provide it as an argument to the index[] operator or the get() method.

For example, here is a dictionary:

```
>>> Jen = {'Name':'Jen Rum', 'Telephone': 18869875674, 'Job':'Secretary'}
```

To access dictionary values one at a time, you will provide the corresponding key inside the square brackets:

```
>>> Jen['Name']
'Jen Rum'

>>> Jen['Telephone']
18869875674

>>> Jen['Job']
'Secretary'
```

To obtain the values using the get() method:

```
>>> Jen.get('Name')
'Jen Rum'

>>> Jen.get('Telephone')
18869875674

>>> Jen.get('Job')
'Secretary'
```

Adding and Modifying Key-Value Pairs

You can add a new dictionary entry or modify an existing one with an assignment statement:

```
mydict [key] = x
```

Whenever a new pair is assigned to a dictionary, Python verifies whether a key is unique or a duplicate of an existing key. If no similar key exists in the dictionary, the new key-value pair is added. If a similar key exists, the existing value is replaced by the new value.

For example, to add a new entry to the Jen dictionary:

>>> Jen['Age'] = 21

If you need to modify a value for an existing key, simply assign a new value:

>>> Jen['Job'] = 'Cashier'

You can view the updated dictionary at this point:

>>> Jen
{'Age': 21, 'Job': 'Cashier', 'Telephone': 18869875674, 'Name': 'Jen Rum'}

Removing or Deleting Elements

The pop() method

The pop() method is used to remove a specific key-value pair and return the deleted value.

For example, to delete the key 'Age' and its corresponding value on the Jen dictionary:

>>> Jen.pop('Age')
21

Here's the output if you try to print the Jen dictionary at this point:

>>> print(Jen)
{'Job': 'Cashier', 'Telephone': 18869875674, 'Name': 'Jen Rum'}

The popitem() method

The popitem() method removes and returns a random key-value pair and takes no argument.

For example, if you use the popitem() method on the Jen dictionary, it will return an arbitrary pair:

```
>>> Jen.popitem()
('Job', 'Cashier')
```

To see the remaining pairs of the dictionary:

```
>>> Jen
{'Telephone': 18869875674, 'Name': 'Jen Rum'}
```


The clear() method

The clear() method is used to remove all items in a dictionary.

To remove the remaining pairs in the Jen dictionary:

```
>>> Jen.clear()
```

At this point, you have an empty dictionary:

```
>>> Jen
{}
```


Deleting a dictionary with the del keyword

To delete the Jen dictionary completely, you will use the del keyword:

>>>del Jen

Other Commonly Used Dictionary Methods

keys()   returns a list of dictionary keys

syntax: dict.keys()

For example:

>>> hobbies = {'a':'painting', 'b':'archery', 'c':'golf', 'd':'paintball'}

To display the keys of the hobbies dictionary:
>>> hobbies.keys()
dict_keys(['a', 'b', 'd', 'c'])

values()   returns a list of dictionary values

syntax: dict.values()

To display the values of the hobbies dictionary:
>>> hobbies.values()
dict_values(['painting', 'archery', 'paintball', 'golf'])

setdefault()

The setdefault() method searches for a specified key and returns its value. If the key is non-existent, it returns the given default value and adds it to the dictionary.

syntax:

dict.setdefault(key, default=None)

For example, to use setdefault() to search for a key in the hobbies dictionary and provide a default value, quilting:

```
>>> hobbies.setdefault('c', 'quilting')
'golf'
```

The method returned 'golf', the value of 'c' and discarded the default value given because the key exists in the dictionary.

To see how Python responds to the method when you specify a non-existent key, use the setdefault() method again:

```
>>> hobbies.setdefault('e', 'quilting')
'quilting'
```

The method returned the value of 'quilting' which means that it updated the dictionary with a new key-value pair. To view the updated hobbies dictionary:

```
{'a': 'painting', 'b': 'archery', 'd': 'paintball', 'c': 'golf', 'e': 'quilting'}
```

update()

The update() method updates a current dictionary with pairs from another dictionary. Take note that when there are common keys between the two dictionaries, the other dictionary's value will overwrite that of the current dictionary.

For example, given are two dictionaries, the base_dict and the other_dict:

```
>>> base_dict = {'animal':'chameleon', 'color':'green',
'habitat':'forest'}
>>> other_dict = {'animal':'chameleon', 'color':'brown',
'lifespan':'10 years'}
```

To update the base_dict with the items on other_dict:

```
>>> base_dict.update(other_dict)
```

To view the updated base_dict:

```
>>> base_dict
{'lifespan': '10 years', 'animal': 'chameleon', 'color': 'brown',
'habitat': 'forest'}
```

Notice that the key 'lifespan' and its corresponding value was added to the base_dict. Likewise, the color was updated from green to brown. Since only the base_dict was updated, the method does not affect the other_dict at all.

To view the other_dict:

```
>>> other_dict
{'lifespan': '10 years', 'animal': 'chameleon', 'color': 'brown'}
```

copy()

The copy() method performs a shallow copy of a dictionary by copying each key-value pair to a new dictionary.

For example, to make a copy of the other_dict above to a new dictionary that will be named exotic_1:

```
>>> exotic_1 = other_dict.copy()
```

To view the new dictionary:

```
>>> exotic_1
{'animal': 'chameleon', 'lifespan': '10 years', 'color': 'brown'}
```

fromkeys()

The fromkeys() method takes items from a sequence-type data such as a list and uses them as keys to build a new dictionary. It takes a second argument which can be used to provide a value that will be associated with the new dictionary keys.

For example, here is a list that can be used to obtain the keys required to create a dictionary:

```
my_list = ['Title', 'Author', 'Publisher', 'Editor']
```

To build a new dictionary, 'pub_dict', from my_list using fromkeys() specifying 'Spiderman' as the default value:

```
>>> pub_dict = dict.fromkeys(my_list, 'Spiderman')
```

Here's the content of the new pub_dict dictionary:

```
>>> pub_dict
{'Author': 'Spiderman', 'Editor': 'Spiderman', 'Publisher': 'Spiderman', 'Title': 'Spiderman'}
```

Chapter 7
Operators

Operators are symbols or special characters that indicate the execution of a specific process. You will use them to assign, evaluate, verify, or perform tasks on variables or data.

Python supports the following operators:

Arithmetic operators
Assignment operators
Comparison or Relational Operators
Membership Operators
Logical Operators

Arithmetic Operators

Addition (+)

The addition operator adds the value of the left and right operands.

```
>>>2+ 6
8
```

Subtraction (-)

The subtraction operator subtracts the value of the right operand from the value of the left operand.

```
>>>22 – 7
15
```

Multiplication (*)

The multiplication operator multiplies the values of the left and right operands.

```
>>>25 * 3
75
```

Division (/)

The division operator divides the value of the left operand with the value of the right operand.

```
>>>60 / 15
4.0
```

Exponent (**)

The exponent operator raises the value of the first operand to the number indicated by the second operand.

```
>>> 3**3
27
```

Modulos (%)

The modulos operator returns the remainder after dividing the number on the left side of the operator by the number on the right.

```
>>> 32 % 5
2
```

Floor Division (//)

The floor division operator divides the value of the left operand by the value of the right operand and returns a quotient as a whole number.

```
>>> 45//4
11
```

Assignment Operators

Assignment operators are used to assign values to variables.

=   Assigns the value of the right operand to the left operand:

```
>>> abc = 'Jack'
```

+= add and

Adds the values of the left and right operands and assigns the sum to the left operand:

```
counter += 10
```

-= subtract and

Subtracts the value of the right operand from the value of the left operand and assigns the difference to the left operand:

```
b -= 3
```

*= multiply and

Multiplies the values of both operands and assigns the product to the left operand:

xyz *= 7

/= divide and

Divides the value of the left operand with the value of the right operand and assigns the quotient to the left operand:

abc /= 3

**= exponent and

Performs exponential calculation on the left operand and assigns the value to the left operand:

y **= 4

%= modulos and

Takes the modulos between the left and right operands and assigns the result to the left operand:

xyz %= 3

//= floor division and

Performs floor division of the operands and assigns the value to the left operand

a //= 2

Relational Operators

Relational operators evaluate the values of the left and right operands and return whether the indicated relation is true or false.

Following are the relational or comparison operators:

==	left operand is equal to the right operand
!=	left operand is not equal to the right operand
>	left operand is greater than the right operand
<	left operand is less than the right operand
>=	left operand is greater than or equal to right operand
<=	left operand is less than or equal to right operand

Examples:
```
>>> xyz = 100
>>> abc = 75
>>> xyz == abc
False
```

Membership Operators

Membership operators check for the occurrence or non-occurrence of a value in a sequence type data or of a key in a dictionary.

in

The 'in' operator returns True if a specified value occurs in a sequence or if a given key is found in a dictionary and returns False if otherwise.

not in

The 'not in' operator returns True if a given value does not occur in a sequence or if a specified key does not appear in dictionary and returns False if otherwise.

Examples:

```
>>> my_list = [1, 4, 6, 8, 12, 24, 20, 'a', 'd', 'e']
>>> 20 in my_list
True
>>> 8 not in my_list
False

>>> member_1 = {'Name':'Martha Swan', 'Age':24,
        'State':'Illinois'}
>>> 'Name' in member_1
True
>>> 'Height' in member_1
False
>>> 'Age' not in member_1
False
```

Logical Operators

There are three logical operators in Python:
and
or
not

Python applies the following rules when evaluating logical expressions:

x and y
The 'and' operator returns True if both arguments are true. It returns False if one argument is false.

x or y
The 'or' operator returns True if at least one of the arguments is True. It returns False if both arguments are false.

not y
The 'not' operator returns True if the argument is false and False if the argument is true.

Examples:

```
>>> a = 5
>>> b = 3
>>> (a > 2) and (b < 12)
True

>>> (a < 2) or (b < 5)
True

>>> (a < 3) and (b == 2)
False


>>> not(a == 3)
True
>>> not(a == 5)
False
```

Chapter 8
Functions and Modules

Functions

A function is a statement or a group of related statements that performs a specific task. Functions are reusable and they help make programming more efficient.

In Python, a function is also an object. Hence, it can be assigned to a variable or passed as an argument.

A function is either built-in or user-defined.

Built-in Functions

Python features the following built-in functions:

abs()	all()	ascii()	any()
bin()	bool()	bytes()	bytearray()
callable()	chr()	compile()	classmethod()
complex()	delattr()	dir()	dict()
divmod()	enumerate()	exec()	eval()
filter()	format()	float()	frozenset()
globals()	getattr()	hasattr()	hash()
hex()	help()	__import__()	id()
input()	int()	issubclass()	isinstance()
iter()	list()	len()	locals()
max()	map()	min()	memoryview()
next()	object()	open()	oct()
ord()	print()	pow()	property()
repr()	range()	round()	reversed()
set()	slice()	setattr()	sorted()

str()	sum()	staticmethod()	super()
type()	tuple()	vars()	zip()

The following are the most commonly used built-in functions:

print()

The print() function prints value to the default output mode, the screen.'

Examples:

>>> print("Python is fun!")
Python is fun!

input()

The input() function reads keyboard input and returns the string.

This function takes an optional parameter, a prompt string, which is displayed whenever the function is called. It returns the user's response as a string.

To illustrate, here is program that asks for user's input:

```
a = input('Please enter your name: ')
print('Hi, ' + a + '!')
num = input('Please enter your student number: ')
print('Your name is ' + a + ' and your student number is ' + num)
```

If you enter James as your name and the number 8765 as your student number, here' how the interaction would appear:

Please enter your name: James
Hi, James!
Please enter your student number: 8675
Your name is James and your student number is 8675.

len()

This function returns the size or length of an object.

To get string size:

```
>>> a = 'pineapple'
>>> len(a)
9

>>> len('programming')
11
```

To get list size:

```
>>> items = ['sheep', 12, 'white', 'cup', 94.2]
>>> len(items)
5
```

To get dictionary size:

```
>>> animal_1 = {'name':'sheep', 'male':'ram', 'female':'ewe',
'young':'lamb'}
>>> len(animal_1)
4
```

max()

The max() function returns the largest item.

```
>>> my_num = [4, 12, 87.5, -150, 90, 24]
>>> max(my_num)
90
```

min()

The min() function returns the smallest item.

```
>>> my_num = [4, 12, 87.5, -150, 90, 24]
>>> min(my_num)
-150
```

abs()

The abs() function returns the absolute value of a number.

```
>>> abs(-5)
5
```

```
>>> x = 3
>>>abs(x)
3
```

round()

The round() function returns the rounded value of a floating point number.

To round off to the nearest digit:

```
>>> round(56.9874560)
57
```

To round off to the nearest 2 decimal places:

```
>>> a = 87.23424
>>> round(a, 2)
87.23
```

type()

The type() function returns the object type of the argument.

```
>>> a = 'primary'
>>> type(a)
<class 'str'>

>>> b = ('p', 'r', 'i', 'm', 'a','r', 'y')
>>> type(b)
<class 'tuple'>

>>> c = [1, 3, 5, 7, 9, 'wall']
>>> type(c)
<class 'list'>

>>> d = {'a':1, 'b':2, 'c':3}
>>> type(d)
<class 'dict'>
```

range()

syntax: range(start, end, step)

The range() function is used to return an iterator or a list with arithmetic progression. It takes a maximum of 3 integer arguments to indicate the start, end, and progression of the sequence. When only one argument is given, it is assigned to the 'end' argument and the 'start' takes the default value of zero while the 'step' or progression defaults to 1.

For example, to return a list from a given range:

```
>>> list(range(10))
[0, 1, 2, 3, 4, 5, 6, 7, 8, 9]

>>> list(range(0, 40, 5))
[0, 5, 10, 15, 20, 25, 30, 35]

>>> new_list = list(range(2, 14, 2))
>>> print(new_list)
[2, 4, 6, 8, 10, 12]
```

list()

The list() function returns a list from a given sequence or dictionary keys:

```
>>> a = 'Programs'
>>> new_list = list(a)
>>> print(new_list)
['P', 'r', 'o', 'g', 'r', 'a', 'm', 's']

>>> dict1 = {'color':'red', 'number':3, 'size':'small'}
>>> my_list = list(dict1)
>>> print(my_list)
['number', 'color', 'size']
```

dict()

The dict() function creates a new dictionary from tuple pairs.

First, you have to create a list of tuple pairs:

>>> pairs_list = [('shape', 'round'), ('size', 'medium'), ('color', 'blue')]

Use the dict() function to convert the list to a dictionary:

>>> my_dict = (dict(pairs_list))

Now, type my_dict to view the new dictionary:

>>> my_dict
{'size': 'medium', 'color': 'blue', 'shape': 'round'}

str()

The str() function is used to return a string from a non-string value.

Example:

>>> name = 'Leila'
>>> age = 26
>>> print('Her name is ' + name + ' and she is ' +str(age) + ' years old.')
Her name is Leila and she is 26 years old.

The str() function explicitly converts the integer into a string literal that can be used for printing. Python will raise a TypeError if you attempt to print the variable 'age' without explicit conversion:

```
>>> print('Her name is ' + name + ' and she is ' + age + '
    years old.')
Traceback (most recent call last):
  File "<pyshell#33>", line 1, in <module>
    print('Her name is ' + name + ' and she is ' + age + ' years
        old.')
TypeError: Can't convert 'int' object to str implicitly
```

User-Defined Functions

User-defined functions are functions created by programmers to perform a specific task. They are created using Python's def keyword.

Syntax:

```
def function_name():
    function body
```

Programmers typically write a docstring at the top of a function's body. Docstrings provide information on what the function does.

The function's body may consist of one statement or a group of statements which must use the same indentation to form a block.

The parameters or arguments are used to pass values to a function and are enclosed in parentheses. A function can take a default or optional argument. A function with a default argument will not require an argument when called. It will return the default value when called without an argument.

To illustrate, here is a simple function:

```
def Greeter(name="Guest"):
    """ Greets users. """
    print("Welcome, " + name + "!")
```

The Greeter function provides an optional argument 'Guest' which will be printed if no argument is given. For example, call the function on the Python prompt with a name argument, 'Gail' by typing Greeter('Gail'):

```
>>> Greeter('Gail')
Welcome, Gail!
```

Now, call the function without providing an argument by simply typing Greeter on the prompt:

```
>>> Greeter()
Welcome, Guest!
```

Notice that calling the Greeter() function without specifying an argument returned the default argument 'Guest'.

Return Statement

A function may or may not return a value. A function may be designed to return a value by including a return statement within its body.

syntax:

return [expression]

Example:

```
def double(num):
    """Return the square of a number."""
    return num**2
```

When you call the function 'double' on the prompt, it will return a value:

```
>>> double(3)
9

>>> double(4)
16
```

Functions with Two or More Arguments

A function can take more than one parameter and each can have its own default argument. When you have a mix of default and non-default arguments, you should always place the non-default argument/s on the left of those with default arguments.

To illustrate, here is a function with three arguments:

```
def Hello(name, title = 'my friend', message = 'Good Day'):
    """ Greets a person and prints a message"""
    print('Hello' , name + ', ' + title + '. ' + message + '!')

Hello('Jamille')
Hello('Jazz', 'my pet', 'Happy Birthday')
```

This time, the function was called within the program. In the first call line, only one argument was supplied. In the second call, all three arguments were supplied. If you run the program, here's what the output would be:

Hello Jamille, my friend. Good Day!
Hello Jazz, my pet. Happy Birthday!

Keyword Arguments

The values you supply on a function call are assigned by default according to the position of the arguments. Hence, when you gave the values 'Jazz', 'my pet, and 'Happy Birthday', these were all assigned to the name, title, and message respectively. You can override the default positional arrangement by using keyword arguments on function call.

A keyword argument is one that assigns a value to the parameter name on function call.

For example, call the 'Hello' function on the prompt with the following arguments:

```
>>> Hello(title='my sweetheart', name='Fleur',
message="Have fun")
Hello Fleur, my sweetheart. Have fun!
```

When you call a function with both positional and keyword arguments, the positional argument/s should always precede the keyword argument.

```
>>> Hello('Fleur', message='Have fun', title='my sweetie')
Hello Fleur, my sweetie. Have fun!
```


Arbitrary Arguments

A program may sometimes require calling a function with an undetermined number of arguments. Python allows the use of arbitrary arguments to facilitate this function.

For example, this function greets any number of people that will be named on the function call:

```
def Greeter(*guests):
    """Greets all guests given in the guests tuple"""

    for x in  guests:
        print("Hello", x)
```

When you call the function on the prompt by providing a tuple of names as arguments:

```
>>> Greeter('Janice', 'Mike', 'Francis', 'Donna', 'Jon')
```

Here's what Python will return:

```
Hello Janice
Hello Mike
Hello Francis
Hello Donna
Hello Jon
```

Functions Calling another Function

A function may also call another function.

Example:

#comp_sum calls the dept_sum function

```
def dept_sum(x):
    return x * 4

def comp_sum(a):
    return dept_sum(a) + 10

print(comp_sum(4))
print(comp_sum(2))
print(comp_sum(9))
```

Here's the output when you run the program:

```
26                    #4 * 4+ 10
18                    #2 * 4 + 10
46                    #9 * 4 + 10
```

Modules

A module is a file that contains statements, definitions, or codes. Python has many built-in modules like math, random, re, calendar, and os modules but you can also create your own module. The use of modules helps make Python programming more efficient by promoting code reusability within and across programs and platforms.

For instance, you can create a module that will contain all functions that you use frequently and simply import the module and the corresponding function or attribute whenever you need it in any of your programs.

To illustrate, create a module that will contain the definitions of the functions double, adder, and multiplier. Save the module as Formula.py:

```python
def double(num):
    """Returns the square of a number."""
    return num**2

def adder(x, y):
    """Adds the values and returns the result."""
    xy = x + y
    return xy

def multiplier(x, y):
    """Multiplies the values and returns the result """
    xy = x * y
    return xy
```

After typing and saving, close the file to prepare it for further processing.

Importing a Module

To be able to use the attributes and functions of a module, you need to import the same to your program or on the prompt.

syntax:

import module

Hence, to import the module formula you created:

import Formula

The import statement places the Formula module in the active memory of the interpreter. You can now make use of the functions stored in the module by applying the dot operator:

```
>>> Formula.double(5)
25

>>> Formula.multiplier(6, 4)
24

>>> Formula.adder(10, 5)
15
```

Built-in Modules

Python has numerous built-in modules that you can import and use in your programs.

Math Module

The math module is one of the most frequently used modules in Python. By importing the math module, you will gain access to its attributes, constants, and a great range of mathematical functions.

To access its attributes and methods, you will use the dot operator on math, specify the method, and provide the parameter.

To illustrate, import the math module:

>>>import math

To view its contents, use the dir keyword on math:

```
>>>dir(math)
['__doc__', '__loader__', '__name__', '__package__',
'__spec__', 'acos', 'acosh', 'asin', 'asinh', 'atan', 'atan2',
'atanh', 'ceil', 'copysign', 'cos', 'cosh', 'degrees', 'e', 'erf', 'erfc',
'exp', 'expm1', 'fabs', 'factorial', 'floor', 'fmod', 'frexp', 'fsum',
'gamma', 'gcd', 'hypot', 'inf', 'isclose', 'isfinite', 'isinf', 'isnan',
'ldexp', 'lgamma', 'log', 'log10', 'log1p', 'log2', 'modf', 'nan',
'pi', 'pow', 'radians', 'sin', 'sinh', 'sqrt', 'tan', 'tanh', 'trunc']
```

To use its methods and attributes:

```
>>> math.sqrt(25)
5.0

>>> math.gcd(5, 20)
5

>>> math.pi
3.141592653589793

>>> math.__doc__
'This module is always available.  It provides access to the\nmathematical functions defined by the C standard.'
```

The Random Module

The random module is commonly used when you want to generate a random item within a specified range. This module contains several methods that are commonly used in games that require users to pick a random item.

To access the module, use the import keyword:

import random

The random module has several useful methods.

randint()

The randint() method takes two arguments and generates a random number. The first argument is the lowest value while the second argument is the highest value that can be returned.

Example:

>>> import random

To return any number from 1 to ten:

>>> print(random.randint(1, 10))
5

choice()

The choice() function generates a random value from a specified sequence:

For example:

import random

```python
items = ['Jackpot!','You lose!', 'Take two chances!', 'Go
home!']

print(random.choice(items))
print(random.choice(items))
print(random.choice(items))
```

If you run the program, you might get the following output:

```
You lose!
Jackpot!
Go home!
```

shuffle

The shuffle() function sorts a list's elements in random order.

syntax:

random.shuffle(list)

Example:

import random

```
num_list = [1, 2, 12, 15, 10, 9, 20]
random.shuffle(num_list)
```

print(num_list)

When you run the program, you might get this result:

[1, 15, 12, 20, 10, 9, 2]

randrange

The randrange() function generates a random element from a specified range.

syntax:

random.randrange(start, stop[, step])

example:

```
import random
for num in range(4):
    print(random.randrange(0, 43, 3))
```

When run, the above code will generate 4 random numbers divisible by 3 like the following combination:

12
42
9
27

Chapter 9
Decision Making

Decision making structures are commonly available in computer languages. They facilitate the implementation of a course of action based on the response to a test condition.

A decision making block starts with a Boolean expression and branches out to another block indicated by either a True or False response.

Python supports these decision making structures:

if statements
if else statements
if...elif...else statements

if statements

syntax:

if condition:
    block

Example:

```
num = int(input("Enter a number: "))
if num >= 10:
    print("Welcome! You belong to the Star Class.")
print("This program classifies members based on user's response.")
```

If the user enters 12, the program prints the statement given under the 'if block':

Enter a number: 12
Welcome! You belong to the Star Class.
This program classifies members based on user's response.

If the user enters a number below 10, like 6, the program proceeds to the next unindented line:

Enter a number: 6
This program classifies members based on user's response.

if...else statements

In if...else structures, Python executes the 'if block' if the test expression generates a True response. Otherwise, if the response is False, it implements the 'else block'.

syntax:

```
if test expression:
    if block

else:
    else block
```

Example:

```
#This program checks if an item is on stock and asks the buyer to pay the indicated price.

items = {'stapler':10, 'paper':5, 'pen':2, 'pencil':2, 'marker':4}

x = input("Please enter your order: ")
if x in items:
    print("You ordered a/an " + x + " and it is on stock. Please pay $" + str(items.get(x)) + '.')
```

else:
    print("Sorry, " + x + " is out of stock.")

If you run the program and responded with paper, maker, and eraser, here are the program's output:

Please enter your order: paper
You ordered a/an paper and it is on stock. Please pay $5.

Please enter your order: marker
You ordered a/an marker and it is on stock. Please pay $4.

Please enter your order: eraser
Sorry, eraser is out of stock.

if...elif...else statements

An if...elif...else structure allows the evaluation of multiple expressions. If the 'if condition' yields True, it executes the 'if block'. If it yields False, it evaluates the 'elif' block. If the 'elif' test expression is True, it executes the 'elif block'. Otherwise, it executes the 'else block'.

syntax:

if test expression:
    if block
elif test expression:
    elif block
else:
    else block

Example:

#This program checks if an item is on stock and asks buyer to pay the indicated price if the item is available.

#If not on stock, it will check if the given item is on the pending order list and prints a remark.
#If the order is neither on stock nor pending, the program prints an appropriate remark.

```python
items = {'stapler':10, 'paper':5, 'pen':2, 'pencil':2, 'marker':4}

pending = ['eraser', 'notebook', 'folder']

x = input("Please enter your order: ")

if x in items:
    print("You ordered a/an " + x + " and it is on stock. Please pay $" + str(items.get(x)) + '.')

elif x in pending:
    print("You ordered a/an " + x + " and it will be delivered tomorrow.")

else:
    print("Sorry, " + x + " is out of stock.")
```

If you run the program and responded with pen, notebook, and clip, here's what the output would be:

Please enter your order: pen
You ordered a/an pen and it is on stock. Please pay $2.

Please enter your order: notebook
You ordered a/an notebook and it will be delivered tomorrow.

Please enter your order: clip
Sorry, clip is out of stock.

Chapter 10
Flow Control

Loops are program control structures that allow intricate execution paths and repetitive execution of a statement or a block of code.

For loop

A 'for loop' is used to iterate over items of sequence data types like strings, lists, or tuples.

syntax:

for val in sequence:
    statement(s)

On a 'for loop', the variable stores the value of each sequence element with every iteration. The loop goes on until all elements are processed.

Examples:

A 'for loop' over a string:

for letter in 'First Class':
    print('<**', letter, '**>')

Here's the output when you run the loop:

<* F *>
<* i *>
<* r *>
<* s *>

```
<* t *>
<*   *>
<* C *>
<* l *>
<* a *>
<* s *>
<* s *>
```

A 'for loop' over a list:

colors = ['yellow', 'blue', 'violet', 'brown', 'black', 'white']

for item in colors:
    print('A ' + item + ' backpack is cool!')
print('These backpacks are amazing!')

When you run the loop, here's what you will get:

A yellow backpack is cool!
A blue backpack is cool!
A violet backpack is cool!
A brown backpack is cool!
A black backpack is cool!
A white backpack is cool!
These backpacks are amazing!

While Loop

The 'while loop' is used when you need to repeatedly execute a statement or block of code while a test condition is True. When it is no longer True, control passes to the next line after the loop.

syntax:

```
while test condition
    statement(s)
```

Example:

```
#program adds number from 1 up to a
#user-provided number
#total = 1+2+3...+ given number

num = int(input("Enter a number: "))

#initialize total and counter
total = 0
counter = 1

while counter <= num:
    total = total + counter
    counter += 1

#print the total
print("The total is: ", total)
```

When you run the program and enter the numbers 3, 5, and 8:

```
Enter a number: 3
The total is:  6

Enter a number: 5
The total is:  15

Enter a number: 8
The total is:  36
```

Break Statement

A break statement terminates the loop and passes control to the next statement after the loop. It ends the iteration regardless of the test expression and prevents the program from running the 'else' statement.

Example:

```
#loop ends upon reaching a specified item

items = ['affordable', 'available', 'suitable', 'used', 'perfect fit']

for x in items:
  if x == 'used':
    break
  print('I love' ,x, 'clothes.')
print("It's Mega Sales season!")
```

Once the loop reaches 'used', it terminates and the program runs the next unindented line.

```
I love affordable clothes.
I love available clothes.
I love suitable clothes.
It's Mega Sales season!
```

Continue Statement

The continue statement tells the program to continue to the next iteration after reaching and skipping a given item in the sequence.

For example, you can replace the break statement with the continue statement in the above example:

```
items = ['affordable', 'available', 'suitable', 'used', 'perfect fit']

for x in items:
  if x == 'used':
    continue
  print('I love' ,x, 'clothes.')
print("It's Mega Sales season!")
```

The loop skips the iteration when it reaches 'used' and proceeds to the next item on the list:

```
I love affordable clothes.
I love available clothes.
I love suitable clothes.
I love perfect fit clothes.
It's Mega Sales season!
```

Pass Statement

A pass is a null operation in Python. The interpreter reads the statement and does nothing. It is commonly used as a placeholder for a statement or block of statements. Programmers use them to enable partial program testing.

```
syntax:
  pass
```

Example:

```
#pass statement in an 'if' structure:

if x in item:
  pass
```

Try and Except Statements

Python has built-in exceptions that cause a program to return an error whenever it runs into a problem. Whenever an error occurs, the process terminates and control is passed to the calling process and to the process before it until it is handled. Failure to manage the error causes a program to crash.

One of the ways to handle program errors and exceptions in Python is with the 'try and except' structure. A critical program segment is placed under the 'try' clause. The statement or group of statements that will handle the error is provided under the 'except' clause.

Example:

```
try:
    xyz = int(input("Please enter a number: "))
    print("You entered %d." % xyz)
except ValueError:
    print("You have entered an invalid character.")
```

Python will try to execute the group of statements under the 'try' clause. This is a critical part of the program as the programmer anticipates that a figure other than a number will be entered by a user and that this might lead to a ValueError. Whenever the program runs into a ValueError, control passes to the 'except' block which handles the error.

For example, if you run the above program using an integer and a letter, you will get the following output:

Please enter a number: 6
You entered 6.

Please enter a number: a
You have entered an invalid character.

Conclusion

I hope that this book was able to help you to learn the fundamentals of Python Programming and motivate you to take a higher leap towards a programming career in Python.

The next step is to optimize your skills and take it to the next level by creating your own programs or acquiring advance programming skills through a professional course.

I wish you the best of luck!

Made in the USA
Middletown, DE
10 October 2020

21550893R00057